CHRIS DEVON

Beginners Blazor Server Guide

Contents

Introduction

Welcome to the world of Blazor Server, a technology that's transforming web development by allowing developers to build interactive, dynamic applications using .NET and C# without the need for JavaScript. This book is crafted as a hands-on, beginner-friendly guide that will take you from the initial setup through advanced Blazor Server topics with practical projects. By the end, you'll have built a series of applications that you can confidently showcase, and you'll have the foundation to explore even more complex .NET and web development challenges.

About This Book

The motivation behind creating this book is simple: Blazor Server is powerful, accessible, and rapidly growing in popularity, but resources for true beginners—especially those looking to build real-world applications—are scarce. You might find yourself combing through disparate tutorials or piecing together solutions on forums, only to end up with more questions than answers. This book aims to bridge that gap by providing a structured learning path focused on real-world applications and best practices, designed to make Blazor Server accessible to anyone with a background in web development or C# programming.

Blazor Server allows you to create single-page applications (SPAs) with all the dynamism and interactivity of JavaScript-based frameworks but without JavaScript itself. For developers rooted in C# or .NET, this is a breakthrough technology that brings the power and productivity of .NET to the browser. In essence, Blazor Server delivers a blend of server-rendered and client-rendered interactivity that feels intuitive and powerful, ideal for both rapid prototyping and large-scale applications.

This book serves as a "crash course," meaning it's intended to provide deep yet accessible insights as efficiently as possible. You won't just learn how to code with Blazor Server; you'll understand how it works, why certain practices are effective, and where Blazor Server fits within the broader web development ecosystem.

Who This Book is For

This book is intended for developers at a variety of experience levels, though a few basic prerequisites will help you get the most out of it:

1. **Web Developers**: If you're experienced with HTML, CSS, and maybe JavaScript but are new to .NET or C#, this book will introduce you to the .NET ecosystem with a focus on Blazor.
2. **C# Developers**: Familiar with C# but new to web development? This book is ideal for guiding you through the world of Blazor Server while giving you a solid foundation in web development concepts.
3. **ASP.NET Developers**: If you've worked with ASP.NET MVC or Web Forms, Blazor Server will feel familiar yet refreshingly modern. This book will help you understand how Blazor Server builds on and differs from traditional ASP.NET approaches.
4. **Self-Learners and Hobbyists**: If you're interested in learning a new skill that combines the power of .NET with the interactivity of modern web apps, you'll find this guide comprehensive and practical.

This book assumes a working knowledge of C# and the basics of web development, such as HTML and CSS. However, each chapter begins with a quick recap or introduction to the core concepts you'll need to proceed.

How to Use This Book

Each chapter in this book introduces a foundational aspect of Blazor Server, gradually building toward more complex, project-based applications. The learning path is intentionally designed to be progressive, meaning it's best to go through the chapters in order. Each chapter introduces concepts that will be applied in the projects you'll build, so completing them sequentially will yield the best results.

- **Chapter Overviews**: Each chapter begins with a brief overview of what you'll learn. This is where we'll frame the topics to help you understand the "why" as well as the "how."
- **Hands-On Code Examples**: Blazor Server is best learned through practice. Expect plenty of code examples with clear explanations. Each example is crafted to help you learn a specific skill that you'll apply in projects later on.
- **Chapter Summaries and Key Takeaways**: At the end of each chapter, you'll find a summary of key points. Use this section to reinforce your understanding before moving on to the next chapter.
- **Projects**: Several chapters culminate in building real-world applications. These projects are designed to synthesize multiple concepts and provide a satisfying sense of accomplishment. By the end of each project, you'll have hands-on experience with Blazor Server that you can readily apply to your own applications.
- **Troubleshooting and Common Pitfalls**: Some chapters have sections dedicated to troubleshooting common errors and understanding why certain approaches work better than others.

This structured approach provides a well-rounded Blazor Server education, but feel free to jump ahead if there are specific features you want to explore first. Blazor Server has a rich set of tools and techniques, and while this book is structured to maximize your learning experience, flexibility is encouraged based on your goals and timeline.

Setting Up Your Development Environment

Before diving into Blazor Server, you'll need a few essential tools installed on your computer:

1. **.NET SDK**: Blazor Server is part of the .NET ecosystem, so having the latest .NET SDK installed is essential. You can download it from the official .NET website. Follow the installer's instructions and make sure everything is set up properly.

2. **Integrated Development Environment (IDE)**: While any text editor can technically handle Blazor, using a powerful IDE like Visual Studio or Visual Studio Code will improve your experience significantly. Visual Studio offers integrated support for Blazor, making it a great choice for beginners.

3. **Creating Your First Blazor Server Project**: With your environment set up, we'll start by creating your first Blazor Server project in Visual Studio or Visual Studio Code. We'll walk through the project structure and identify key files like the _Imports.razor file, which streamlines component usage, and the Program.cs file, which configures the app at startup.

Each of these setup steps will be covered in detail in the next chapter, where we'll also introduce you to the fundamentals of Blazor Server and build a small app to familiarize you with the environment.

What You Will Build in This Book

To make learning Blazor Server practical and rewarding, this book includes multiple hands-on projects that reflect real-world applications. By the end of this book, you will have built the following:

1. **To-Do List App**: A simple project to introduce core Blazor Server concepts, such as components, data binding, and event handling. You'll start by creating a basic application that captures user input, displays lists, and learns about Blazor's component lifecycle.

2. **Task Manager Application**: This project introduces component lifecycle events, forms and validation, and state management. You'll create a task management application with features like adding, editing, and deleting tasks.

3. **Blog Application**: With this project, you'll dive into data access and APIs. You'll create a simple blog where users can read posts, interact with data using Entity Framework Core, and manage CRUD (Create, Read, Update, Delete) operations.

4. **Real-Time Notification Dashboard**: A more advanced project that incorporates real-time communication using SignalR, a library for creating real-time applications. You'll build a dashboard that displays notifications and updates as they happen, ideal for scenarios like messaging or alerts.

5. **Sales Dashboard**: This project integrates multiple ASP.NET services, allowing you to apply advanced data integration techniques. You'll build a sales dashboard that dynamically updates data, showcases analytics, and emphasizes performance optimization strategies.

These projects are designed to be approachable for beginners while still giving you practical experience. By the end of this book, you'll have the skills to apply Blazor Server in various contexts, from small projects to more sophisticated applications.

Final Thoughts

Blazor Server is a versatile framework with a robust feature set, allowing you to create rich, interactive web applications with the familiarity and strength of .NET. Mastering this technology not only enhances your capabilities as a developer but also opens new doors for creating highly interactive web applications.

This book is your guide to harnessing the potential of Blazor Server. It's about building competence through practical applications, from understanding the basics to developing deployable applications. By investing your time here, you're setting yourself up for a future where Blazor Server, and .NET in general, are powerful tools in your development arsenal.

Now, let's get started with the journey of learning and mastering Blazor Server. The first chapter will introduce you to Blazor's core concepts and set up your first project—an essential first step on the road to proficiency in

Blazor development.

Getting Started with Blazor Server

B lazor Server is part of a powerful set of technologies from Microsoft, built on .NET, that lets developers create interactive, client-side web applications with C#. If you've been building websites using JavaScript frameworks, you may find Blazor Server's approach refreshing, as it enables you to create responsive applications without relying on JavaScript for interactivity. In this chapter, we'll explore what Blazor is, why Blazor Server is an exciting choice, and how to set up your development environment. Then, you'll build your first Blazor Server application, getting familiar with its structure and core elements along the way.

What is Blazor?

Blazor is a .NET-based web framework that brings C# into web development. It's a new way of thinking for many developers accustomed to JavaScript or similar scripting languages. The name *Blazor* itself is a portmanteau of "Browser" and "Razor" (ASP.NET's syntax for combining HTML and C#). In Blazor, C# runs on the client, thanks to WebAssembly, or on the server, depending on which flavor you choose.

Blazor comes in two main hosting models:

1. **Blazor WebAssembly**: Runs C# code in the browser through WebAssembly, enabling true client-side applications without server dependency once the app is loaded.
2. **Blazor Server**: The focus of this book, runs C# code on the server and uses SignalR (a library for real-time web functionality) to synchronize

user actions and UI updates between the server and the client. This model provides quick load times and centralizes processing on the server, making it ideal for many enterprise scenarios.

Blazor Server Pros and Cons

Choosing Blazor Server offers some clear advantages, along with considerations:

- **Pros**:
- **Instant Load Times**: Since only a thin layer is served to the client, Blazor Server apps load quickly, making them feel snappy and responsive.
- **Single Language Stack**: You use C# for both backend and frontend code, reducing complexity and avoiding the need to learn JavaScript.
- **Real-Time Interaction**: Blazor Server uses SignalR to maintain a live connection, enabling real-time updates from server to client, which is useful for dashboards, notifications, and chat applications.
- **Cons**:
- **Requires a Persistent Connection**: Since the server and client stay connected, the user experience depends on a reliable internet connection.
- **Scalability Considerations**: For very high-traffic applications, SignalR connections can impact server performance. Careful state management and scaling strategies can help mitigate this.

Understanding these trade-offs will help you make informed decisions when considering Blazor Server for your projects.

Why Blazor Server for Beginners?

Blazor Server is particularly friendly for beginners because it removes some of the complexities associated with client-side JavaScript frameworks. If you're comfortable with C#, Blazor Server lets you stay within the .NET ecosystem. It also simplifies certain aspects of web development, such as managing state between components or handling browser events, since it leverages .NET's familiar structure and object-oriented principles.

For developers interested in building single-page applications (SPAs) without managing separate stacks for frontend and backend, Blazor Server provides a streamlined solution that lets you focus on building features rather than wrangling technology.

Your First Blazor Server Application

Let's dive in by creating a simple Blazor Server application. This initial project will introduce you to the essential components and show how they work together to render interactive web pages.

Setting Up Your Development Environment

To start building with Blazor Server, make sure you have the following tools installed:

1. **.NET SDK**: Download the latest version of the .NET SDK from Microsoft's official site. The .NET SDK provides all the libraries and tools needed to build and run .NET applications.
2. **Integrated Development Environment (IDE)**: Visual Studio or Visual Studio Code is recommended. Visual Studio offers a comprehensive suite with Blazor support out of the box, while Visual Studio Code is a lighter option that works well for Blazor development.

Once your IDE and SDK are installed, open your IDE, and let's create your first Blazor Server app.

Creating a Blazor Server Project

1. **Open Visual Studio** and select **Create a new project**.
2. Choose **Blazor Server App** from the list of project templates.
3. Click **Next**, name your project (e.g., "BlazorHelloWorld"), and select the desired location for your project files.
4. Select **.NET 7** or the latest version and choose **Create**.

Visual Studio will generate the initial structure for your Blazor Server app. Let's explore this structure and identify key files.

Anatomy of a Blazor Server Project

When you open your new Blazor Server project, you'll see a range of folders and files. Here's a breakdown of the most important ones:

- **Pages Folder**: Contains Razor components that define the UI for each page in your application. Razor components (files with the .razor extension) are a core feature of Blazor and enable you to combine HTML markup with C# code.
- For example, Index.razor is the default homepage of the app, containing HTML and C# code mixed in Razor syntax.
- **Shared Folder**: This folder stores reusable components, such as layout files, headers, and footers. For instance, the MainLayout.razor file defines the overall layout for your app.
- **_Imports.razor**: This file is a Razor-specific feature that allows you to import namespaces globally across components, saving you from having to repeat imports in each component file.
- **Program.cs**: The application's entry point. Here, the app's services are configured, including routing and dependency injection settings. It sets up the app to be hosted as a Blazor Server app.
- **appsettings.json**: This is a common configuration file in .NET applications, used for storing application settings and connection strings. It's a great place to store app-specific data in JSON format.

Understanding the Blazor Server Lifecycle

In Blazor Server, each component follows a lifecycle, and understanding this cycle is crucial for managing state and UI rendering effectively. Here's a basic overview of the key lifecycle methods:

- **OnInitialized**: This method is called when the component is first initialized. It's a good place to set up initial data or make the first API call.
- **OnParametersSet**: This method is invoked whenever the component's parameters change. It's particularly useful if the component receives new

data from a parent component.

- **OnAfterRender**: This method is called after the component has rendered its content to the DOM. It's useful for executing JavaScript interop calls that need to run after rendering.

You'll work with these methods extensively in later projects, but even this initial understanding will help you manage component interactions effectively as you build applications.

Building Your First Application: "Hello World" with Blazor Server

Now that you understand the project structure, let's modify your app to display a simple "Hello World" message.

- **Open** Pages/Index.razor: This file is the default starting point of your application.
- **Edit the Content**:

```
@page "/"

<h1>Hello, Blazor Server!</h1>

@code {
    // This section can hold C# code
}
```

- **Run the Application**: Click the **Run** button (or press F5) in Visual Studio to launch your app. It should open in your default browser, and you'll see the "Hello, Blazor Server!" message displayed.

This simple example introduces you to the Razor syntax, where @ signifies C# code within HTML markup. As you progress, you'll see how Blazor enables seamless integration of C# and HTML to create dynamic, data-driven web pages.

Exploring More with Data Binding and Event Handling

Data binding is a fundamental feature in Blazor Server, allowing you to connect the user interface to your application's data. Let's extend our "Hello World" application by adding a simple form to capture and display user input.

- **Modify** Index.razor to include a text input and a button:

```
@page "/"

<h1>Welcome to Blazor Server</h1>

<p>Enter your name:</p>
<input @bind="name" />

<button @onclick="ShowMessage">Greet Me</button>

<p>@message</p>

@code {
    private string name = "";
    private string message = "";

    private void ShowMessage()
    {
        message = $"Hello, {name}!";
    }
}
```

- **Explanation of Code**:
- The @bind directive connects the name variable to the input field, allowing two-way data binding. This means that any change in the input field automatically updates the name variable.
- The @onclick directive binds the button's click event to the ShowMessage

method. When the button is clicked, ShowMessage sets the message variable, which is displayed in the <p> tag below.

- **Run the App Again**:

Launch the app to test the new functionality. Enter a name, click "Greet Me," and see the personalized greeting displayed.

This example illustrates Blazor Server's data binding and event handling capabilities, essential tools for building interactive web applications.

Key Takeaways

- **Blazor Server** provides a streamlined way to build interactive web applications using C#, eliminating the need for JavaScript for many common tasks.
- **Project Structure**: Familiarizing yourself with the default Blazor Server project structure is crucial. Key files include Index.razor for the homepage, _Imports.razor for shared imports, and Program.cs for configuration.
- **Basic Components**: Creating a "Hello World" app introduced Razor components, data binding, and event handling, foundational concepts for building more complex applications.
- **Lifecycle Awareness**: Understanding Blazor's component lifecycle (e.g., OnInitialized, OnParametersSet) will be beneficial for managing data and interactions as you build more complex applications.

Core Concepts of Blazor Server

With your initial project behind you, it's time to dig into the foundational building blocks of Blazor Server. In this chapter, we'll explore components, data binding, and event handling—three cornerstones of any Blazor application. You'll also gain an understanding of dependency injection, an important design pattern in Blazor Server that allows you to share data and services across components efficiently. We'll wrap up the chapter by building a simple to-do list application, giving you a chance to apply these concepts in a practical way.

Components in Blazor Server

In Blazor Server, components are the essential units of UI. Each component is a self-contained piece of user interface with its own logic, structure, and data. Components can be as simple as a button or as complex as an entire page, and they're typically built using Razor syntax, which combines HTML with C# code.

Understanding Razor Components

A Razor component is defined in a .razor file. Each component can:

- **Render HTML**: Components can output static and dynamic HTML, making it easy to define UI layouts.
- **Contain C# Code**: Using @code blocks, you can include C# code directly in components, giving them interactivity and functionality.
- **Receive and Pass Data**: Components can receive data from their parent components and pass data to other components, enabling complex data

flows.

Creating a New Component

Let's create a component called Greeting.razor to understand the basics of component creation. This component will accept a name as input and display a personalized greeting.

- **Create a New Component File**: In your **Pages** or **Shared** folder, create a new file named Greeting.razor.
- **Define Component Markup and Code**:

```
@code {
    [Parameter]
    public string Name { get; set; }

    private string GreetingMessage => $"Hello, {Name}!";
}

<h2>@GreetingMessage</h2>
```

- **Explanation of Code**:
- [Parameter]: This attribute allows the Name property to be set by the parent component, enabling data to flow into Greeting.
- GreetingMessage Property: This read-only property uses Name to display a personalized message.
- **Use the Component**: In another component, like Index.razor, you can now use <Greeting Name="Blazor Learner" /> to render a personalized greeting.

Component Communication and Reusability

Components can communicate with each other via parameters, events, and cascading parameters. For example, you can pass data down to child components using [Parameter] properties, as shown above. In more advanced scenarios, child components can trigger events that parent components can handle, enabling two-way communication.

Data Binding in Blazor Server

Data binding is a technique that connects the data in your code with your UI elements, creating a "live" link between them. Blazor Server supports several types of data binding, including one-way and two-way binding, making it easy to build interactive applications.

One-Way Binding

One-way binding flows data from your code to the UI, so that when a property changes, the UI is updated automatically.

Example:

```
<h1>@title</h1>

@code {
    private string title = "Welcome to Blazor!";
}
```

In this example, any change to title in the code will automatically reflect in the UI.

Two-Way Binding

Two-way binding allows the UI to update your code as well. It's particularly useful for input fields, where you want to update a variable based on user input.

Example:

```
<input @bind="username" />
<p>Hello, @username!</p>

@code {
    private string username = "";
}
```

With @bind, any text entered in the input field updates the username variable, and changes to username are also reflected in the input field.

Event Handling in Blazor

Event handling allows you to capture and respond to user interactions, such as clicks, mouse movements, and keyboard inputs. In Blazor, event handling is done with @on<EventName> syntax, where <EventName> is the specific event type.

Example: Handling Button Clicks

```
<button @onclick="ShowGreeting">Click Me</button>
<p>@message</p>

@code {
    private string message = "";

    private void ShowGreeting()
    {
        message = "Hello, Blazor!";
    }
}
```

When the button is clicked, ShowGreeting is called, and the message updates. This approach, where UI events trigger code execution, creates a dynamic user experience.

Dependency Injection (DI) Basics

Dependency Injection (DI) is a design pattern widely used in Blazor Server to manage data and services across components in a structured way. DI allows you to "inject" a dependency into a component, so it has access to the resources it needs without directly creating instances.

Blazor Server uses DI to provide access to services such as HTTP clients, configuration settings, and custom data repositories.

Using Dependency Injection in Blazor Server

1. **Registering Services**: Services must be registered with the DI container,

typically in Program.cs. For instance, builder.Services.AddSingleton<M yService>(); makes MyService available to all components.

2. **Injecting Services into Components**:

```
@inject MyService myService

<p>@myService.GetData()</p>

@code {
    // Service usage happens within component logic
}
```

In this example, MyService is injected into the component, allowing it to access GetData() directly.

Project: Building a Simple To-Do List

Let's put these concepts into practice by creating a basic to-do list application. This project will help reinforce component creation, data binding, event handling, and DI.

Project Requirements

The to-do list will allow users to:

- Add new items to the list.
- Mark items as complete.
- Delete items.

Step 1: Set Up the To-Do Model

Define a model for each to-do item in a new file, ToDoItem.cs, in the **Data** folder.

```
public class ToDoItem
{
```

```
public string Title { get; set; }
public bool IsCompleted { get; set; }
}
```

This simple model contains two properties: Title, for the task name, and IsCompleted, a Boolean indicating whether the item is done.

Step 2: Create a Service to Manage To-Do Items

Add a ToDoService.cs file in the **Services** folder. This service will handle operations for adding, updating, and deleting items.

```
using System.Collections.Generic;

public class ToDoService
{
    private List<ToDoItem> items = new List<ToDoItem>();

    public List<ToDoItem> GetItems() => items;

    public void AddItem(ToDoItem item) => items.Add(item);

    public void RemoveItem(ToDoItem item) => items.Remove(item);
}
```

Then, register ToDoService in Program.cs to make it available through DI:

```
builder.Services.AddSingleton<ToDoService>();
```

Step 3: Build the To-Do Component

Create a new component named ToDoList.razor in the **Pages** folder. This component will render the list of items and provide options to add or remove items.

```
@inject ToDoService ToDoService
```

```
<h3>To-Do List</h3>

<input @bind="newItemTitle" placeholder="Add new task" />
<button @onclick="AddItem">Add</button>

<ul>
    @foreach (var item in ToDoService.GetItems())
    {
        <li>
            <input type="checkbox" @bind="item.IsCompleted" />
            @item.Title
            <button @onclick="() =>
            RemoveItem(item)">Delete</button>
        </li>
    }
</ul>

@code {
    private string newItemTitle = "";

    private void AddItem()
    {
        if (!string.IsNullOrWhiteSpace(newItemTitle))
        {
            ToDoService.AddItem(new ToDoItem { Title =
            newItemTitle });
            newItemTitle = "";  // Reset input
        }
    }

    private void RemoveItem(ToDoItem item)
    {
        ToDoService.RemoveItem(item);
    }
}
```

Explanation of Code

- **Adding a New Item**: The AddItem method creates a new ToDoItem with the entered title and adds it to the list using ToDoService.

- **Marking Items Complete**: The checkbox updates the IsCompleted property for each item, thanks to two-way binding with @bind.
- **Deleting an Item**: Each item has a delete button that calls RemoveItem, removing it from the list.

Step 4: Run the Application

Open Index.razor and add the <ToDoList /> component to display it on the homepage. Run the app, and you should see your to-do list in action, allowing you to add, mark complete, and delete tasks.

Key Takeaways

- **Components**: Blazor Server's building blocks. Components can receive data, render HTML, and communicate with other components, making them flexible and reusable.
- **Data Binding**: Blazor Server supports one-way and two-way data binding, allowing UI elements and data to stay in sync.
- **Event Handling**: User interactions, like button clicks, are handled via event handlers, making applications interactive.
- **Dependency Injection**: A pattern that lets you inject services into components, promoting reusability and structured data handling.

Advanced Blazor Server Concepts

As you deepen your knowledge of Blazor Server, it's essential to understand its more advanced features to build dynamic, interactive, and scalable applications. This chapter focuses on key areas that enable Blazor applications to handle complex scenarios and real-time interactions. Mastering these concepts will set you up to create robust applications that effectively manage state, handle user inputs, and optimize performance.

Component Lifecycle and Lifecycle Events

Understanding the lifecycle of a component is crucial for managing data, handling events, and optimizing performance. Blazor Server provides several lifecycle methods that allow you to control how components initialize, update, and render.

Lifecycle Methods in Blazor Server

1. **OnInitialized**: This method is called when the component is initialized, which makes it ideal for setting up initial values or making asynchronous calls.
2. **OnParametersSet**: Invoked whenever the component's parameters are set or updated, OnParametersSet is useful for re-initializing data when the input parameters change.
3. **OnAfterRender**: This method is called after each time the component renders. It's helpful for any code that needs to interact with the rendered DOM, such as JavaScript interop.

4. **Dispose**: Used to release any resources when the component is removed from the UI, Dispose is essential for avoiding memory leaks in long-running applications.

Using Lifecycle Methods in Practice

Let's illustrate these concepts with a component that fetches data when initialized and updates whenever parameters change.

- **Create a New Component**: In the **Pages** folder, add DataDisplay.razor.
- **Add Lifecycle Methods**:

```
@page "/datadisplay/{id:int}"
<h3>Data Display for ID: @Id</h3>

<p>@data</p>

@code {
    [Parameter]
    public int Id { get; set; }

    private string data;

    protected override async Task OnInitializedAsync()
    {
        data = await FetchData(Id);
    }

    protected override async Task OnParametersSetAsync()
    {
        data = await FetchData(Id);
    }

    private Task<string> FetchData(int id)
    {
        // Simulate data fetching
        return Task.FromResult($"Data for ID {id}");
```

```
        }
    }
```

- **Explanation**:
- OnInitializedAsync fetches data the first time the component renders.
- OnParametersSetAsync re-fetches data each time the Id parameter changes, ensuring the component is always displaying up-to-date information.

Lifecycle events help manage data efficiently, ensuring that components fetch or update only as needed, which is crucial in large applications.

State Management in Blazor Server

In single-page applications (SPAs) like those built with Blazor, managing state—i.e., data that persists across different parts of the application—is a core challenge. Blazor Server provides various ways to handle state, from component-level state to session-based storage for data that needs to persist across the application.

Component-Level State

At the simplest level, state can be managed within individual components. However, when data needs to be shared across multiple components, you'll need more advanced techniques.

Using Cascading Parameters for Shared State

Cascading parameters allow a parent component to share data with its child components without having to pass it explicitly through parameters, which is useful when multiple components need access to the same data.

Example:

- **Define the Cascading Parameter** in a parent component:

```
<CascadingValue Value="sharedData">
    <ChildComponent />
</CascadingValue>

@code {
    private string sharedData = "Hello from Parent!";
}
```

- **Access the Cascading Parameter** in ChildComponent.razor:

```
@CascadingParameter
public string SharedData { get; set; }

<p>Data from Parent: @SharedData</p>
```

Cascading parameters make it easy to share data and avoid cluttered code with redundant parameter passing.

Session-Based State Management

For data that needs to persist across multiple pages and refreshes, you can use the ProtectedSessionStorage service, which securely stores data on the server for each user session.

Example:

```
@inject ProtectedSessionStorage sessionStorage

<button @onclick="SaveData">Save Data</button>
<button @onclick="LoadData">Load Data</button>
<p>@data</p>

@code {
    private string data;

    private async Task SaveData()
    {
```

```
        await sessionStorage.SetAsync("key", "Stored Data");
    }

    private async Task LoadData()
    {
        data = await sessionStorage.GetAsync<string>("key");
    }
}
```

Session storage is helpful when you need data to persist temporarily for a specific user session, such as user preferences or application state.

Routing in Blazor Server

Routing in Blazor Server enables navigation within single-page applications by mapping URLs to components. This allows users to move between pages without full page reloads, creating a smooth and responsive experience.

Defining Routes

Each component with a route is assigned a @page directive, where you can define dynamic routes using parameters.

Example of a Simple Route:

```
@page "/products"
<h1>Products</h1>
```

Dynamic Route with Parameter:

```
@page "/products/{id:int}"
<h1>Product Details</h1>

@code {
    [Parameter]
    public int Id { get; set; }
}
```

Using Route Parameters

When defining routes with parameters, Blazor Server allows you to capture and use these values within the component, enhancing navigation flexibility and enabling dynamic page content.

Example of Multiple Parameters:

```
@page "/orders/{orderId:int}/{userId:int}"
<h1>Order Details</h1>
<p>Order ID: @orderId</p>
<p>User ID: @userId</p>

@code {
    [Parameter]
    public int orderId { get; set; }
    [Parameter]
    public int userId { get; set; }
}
```

Routes with multiple parameters enable fine-grained control over navigation paths, which is especially useful for applications with complex data hierarchies.

Forms and Validations

Forms are critical for capturing user input, and Blazor Server provides powerful tools for managing form fields, including validation that ensures data is correct before submission.

Basic Form Structure

A basic form in Blazor consists of input fields wrapped in <EditForm> with Model specifying the object bound to the form.

Example:

```
<EditForm Model="user" OnValidSubmit="HandleSubmit">
    <DataAnnotationsValidator />
    <ValidationSummary />

    <InputText id="username" @bind-Value="user.Username" />
```

```
    <p>@context.Name</p>

    <button type="submit">Submit</button>
</EditForm>

@code {
    private UserModel user = new UserModel();

    private void HandleSubmit()
    {
        // Handle form submission
    }
}
```

Project: Task Manager Application

Let's create a task manager to demonstrate the advanced features covered in this chapter, focusing on state management, routing, lifecycle methods, and forms with validation.

Project Requirements

This app will enable users to:

- Add tasks with a description, priority, and due date.
- Mark tasks as complete.
- Delete tasks.
- Use navigation to view tasks by status (e.g., All, Completed, Pending).

Step 1: Define the Task Model

In the **Data** folder, create a TaskItem.cs file:

```
using System.ComponentModel.DataAnnotations;

public class TaskItem
{
    public int Id { get; set; }
```

```
    [Required]
    public string Description { get; set; }

    [Required]
    [Range(1, 5)]
    public int Priority { get; set; }

    public DateTime DueDate { get; set; }
    public bool IsCompleted { get; set; }
}
```

Step 2: Create the Task Service

Create a TaskService.cs in the **Services** folder to manage tasks.

```
using System.Collections.Generic;

public class TaskService
{
    private List<TaskItem> tasks = new List<TaskItem>();

    public List<TaskItem> GetTasks() => tasks;
    public void AddTask(TaskItem task) => tasks.Add(task);
    public void RemoveTask(TaskItem task) => tasks.Remove(task);
}
```

Register TaskService in Program.cs to make it available for DI:

```
builder.Services.AddSingleton<TaskService>();
```

Step 3: Build the Task Manager Component

Create a new component TaskManager.razor to display the list of tasks and handle task addition.

```
@page "/tasks"
@inject TaskService taskService
```

```
<h3>Task Manager</h3>

<EditForm Model="newTask" OnValidSubmit="AddTask">
   <DataAnnotationsValidator />
   <ValidationSummary />

   <label>Task Description:</label>
   <InputText @bind-Value="newTask.Description" />

   <label>Priority (1-5):</label>
   <InputNumber @bind-Value="newTask.Priority" />

   <label>Due Date:</label>
   <InputDate @bind-Value="newTask.DueDate" />

   <button type="submit">Add Task</button>
</EditForm>

<ul>
   @foreach (var task in taskService.GetTasks())
   {
       <li>
           <input type="checkbox" @bind="task.IsCompleted" />
           @task.Description
           <button @onclick="() =>
           RemoveTask(task)">Delete</button>
       </li>
   }
</ul>

@code {
   private TaskItem newTask = new TaskItem();

   private void AddTask()
   {
       taskService.AddTask(new Task { Description =
       newTask.Description, Priority = newTask.Priority, DueDate =
       newTask.DueDate });
       newTask = new TaskItem(); // Reset form
```

```
    }

    private void RemoveTask(TaskItem task) =>
    taskService.RemoveTask(task);
}
```

Explanation of Code

- **Form Validation**: Uses DataAnnotationsValidator to validate form fields based on [Required] and [Range] attributes in the model.
- **Routing**: Allows users to navigate to /tasks to view the task manager.
- **Session-Based State Management**: The TaskService is registered as a singleton, allowing data to persist across the application.

Key Takeaways

- **Lifecycle Methods**: Provide control over how and when components are initialized, updated, and disposed.
- **State Management**: From cascading parameters to session storage, Blazor Server offers tools to manage and share data effectively.
- **Routing and Parameterized URLs**: Enable smooth in-app navigation with route parameters to display dynamic content.
- **Forms and Validation**: Capture user input and enforce rules using Blazor's validation capabilities.

Working with Data and APIs

Blazor Server's capabilities are magnified when it interacts with databases and APIs. Whether you're fetching data from an external service or connecting to an internal database, understanding how to manage data is essential for creating meaningful applications. This chapter will cover data integration using Entity Framework Core, connecting to APIs, and performing CRUD (Create, Read, Update, Delete) operations, culminating in a practical project where you'll build a simple blog application.

Data Access with Entity Framework Core

Entity Framework Core (EF Core) is an ORM (Object-Relational Mapper) that simplifies data access by abstracting database operations into code. This allows you to interact with databases using C# objects and LINQ queries rather than SQL, making data access code easier to read, maintain, and scale.

Setting Up Entity Framework Core

To start using EF Core in a Blazor Server project, you need to install the necessary NuGet packages. Open the NuGet Package Manager in Visual Studio and add:

- Microsoft.EntityFrameworkCore
- Microsoft.EntityFrameworkCore.SqlServer (or another provider, depending on your database)

Once installed, you're ready to define your data models and context.

Creating a Data Model and Context

Let's define a simple data model for a blog post. In the **Data** folder, create a new class BlogPost.cs.

BlogPost.cs:

```
using System;
using System.ComponentModel.DataAnnotations;

public class BlogPost
{
    public int Id { get; set; }

    [Required]
    public string Title { get; set; }

    public string Content { get; set; }

    public DateTime PublishedDate { get; set; }
}
```

This BlogPost class represents a table in your database where each property corresponds to a column.

Next, define the database context by creating a BlogDbContext.cs class in the **Data** folder. This context serves as the bridge between your data models and the database.

BlogDbContext.cs:

```
using Microsoft.EntityFrameworkCore;

public class BlogDbContext : DbContext
{
    public BlogDbContext(DbContextOptions<BlogDbContext> options)
    : base(options) { }

    public DbSet<BlogPost> BlogPosts { get; set; }
}
```

The DbContext manages interactions with the database, and the DbSet<Blog-Post> property represents a table of BlogPost entries.

Registering the Database Context

To complete the setup, register BlogDbContext in Program.cs so that it can be injected throughout your application. You'll also need to specify the connection string to your database.

- Open Program.cs and add the following:

```
builder.Services.AddDbContext<BlogDbContext>(options =>
    options.UseSqlServer("Your_Connection_String"));
```

- Replace "Your_Connection_String" with the actual connection string for your SQL Server instance.

Once this is done, your application is configured to interact with a SQL database using EF Core.

Integrating External APIs

Blazor Server allows seamless communication with external APIs, making it easy to fetch data from services or expose your application's data through RESTful APIs. To make HTTP requests in Blazor, you'll use the HttpClient class, which provides methods for sending HTTP requests and receiving HTTP responses.

Injecting and Configuring HttpClient

By default, Blazor Server provides an HttpClient that you can inject into components. However, you might want to configure it with base URLs or headers for specific use cases.

- Register HttpClient in Program.cs:

```
builder.Services.AddHttpClient("apiClient", client =>
{
    client.BaseAddress = new Uri("https://api.example.com/");
});
```

- In a component, inject HttpClient:

```
@inject IHttpClientFactory HttpClientFactory

@code {
    private HttpClient client;

    protected override void OnInitialized()
    {
        client = HttpClientFactory.CreateClient("apiClient");
    }
}
```

Making API Requests

To retrieve data, use methods like GetAsync, PostAsync, PutAsync, and DeleteAsync, each of which corresponds to common HTTP verbs.

Example: Fetching Data with GetAsync

```
@inject HttpClient Http

<p>@apiData</p>

@code {
    private string apiData;

    protected override async Task OnInitializedAsync()
    {
        var response = await Http.GetStringAsync("api/resource");
        apiData = response;
```

```
        }
}
```

This approach allows you to fetch data from external services and display it in your components.

CRUD Operations with EF Core

CRUD operations are fundamental to any data-driven application, enabling the creation, retrieval, updating, and deletion of data. EF Core simplifies these operations with a high-level API that allows you to interact with databases as though you're manipulating objects in memory.

Creating Data (Insert)

To add a new record to your database, instantiate the entity, add it to the DbSet, and call SaveChanges to commit the transaction.

Example:

```
var newPost = new BlogPost { Title = "New Post", Content =
"Content", PublishedDate = DateTime.Now };
dbContext.BlogPosts.Add(newPost);
await dbContext.SaveChangesAsync();
```

Reading Data (Select)

Fetching data from the database typically involves querying DbSet using LINQ. Here's an example that retrieves all blog posts ordered by their PublishedDate.

Example:

```
var posts = await dbContext.BlogPosts
    .OrderByDescending(post => post.PublishedDate)
    .ToListAsync();
```

Updating Data (Update)

To update a record, retrieve it, modify its properties, and call SaveChanges.

Example:

```
var post = await dbContext.BlogPosts.FindAsync(postId);
if (post != null)
{
    post.Title = "Updated Title";
    await dbContext.SaveChangesAsync();
}
```

Deleting Data (Delete)

Deleting records is similar: locate the entity, remove it from the DbSet, and call SaveChanges.

Example:

```
var post = await dbContext.BlogPosts.FindAsync(postId);
if (post != null)
{
    dbContext.BlogPosts.Remove(post);
    await dbContext.SaveChangesAsync();
}
```

Project: Creating a Blog Application

Let's bring these concepts together with a blog application that enables users to view, add, edit, and delete blog posts. This project will demonstrate data access, CRUD operations, and API integration.

Step 1: Define the Blog Post Model

You've already defined the BlogPost model in the **Data** folder with properties like Id, Title, Content, and PublishedDate.

Step 2: Create the Blog Service

Create a BlogService class in the **Services** folder to handle data operations for blog posts.

BlogService.cs:

```
public class BlogService
{
```

```csharp
    private readonly BlogDbContext dbContext;

    public BlogService(BlogDbContext dbContext)
    {
        this.dbContext = dbContext;
    }

    public async Task<List<BlogPost>> GetPostsAsync() => await
dbContext.BlogPosts.ToListAsync();

    public async Task<BlogPost> GetPostByIdAsync(int id) => await
dbContext.BlogPosts.FindAsync(id);

    public async Task AddPostAsync(BlogPost post)
    {
        dbContext.BlogPosts.Add(post);
        await dbContext.SaveChangesAsync();
    }

    public async Task UpdatePostAsync(BlogPost post)
    {
        dbContext.BlogPosts.Update(post);
        await dbContext.SaveChangesAsync();
    }

    public async Task DeletePostAsync(int id)
    {
        var post = await dbContext.BlogPosts.FindAsync(id);
        if (post != null)
        {
            dbContext.BlogPosts.Remove(post);
            await dbContext.SaveChangesAsync();
        }
    }
}
```

Register BlogService in Program.cs:

```csharp
builder.Services.AddScoped<BlogService>();
```

Step 3: Create the Blog Components

Create BlogList.razor to display all blog posts and BlogDetails.razor to view individual posts. These components will allow users to read, add, edit, and delete posts.

BlogList.razor:

```
@page "/blogs"
@inject BlogService blogService

<h3>Blog Posts</h3>

<ul>
    @foreach (var post in posts)
    {
        <li>
            <a href="/blogs/@post.Id">@post.Title</a>
            <button @onclick="() =>
            DeletePost(post.Id)">Delete</button>
        </li>
    }
</ul>

@code {
    private List<BlogPost> posts = new();

    protected override async Task OnInitializedAsync()
    {
        posts = await blogService.GetPostsAsync();
    }

    private async Task DeletePost(int id)
    {
        await blogService.DeletePostAsync(id);
        posts = await blogService.GetPostsAsync();
    }
}
```

BlogDetails.razor:

```
@page "/blogs/{id:int}"
@inject BlogService blogService

<h3>@post.Title</h3>
<p>@post.Content</p>
<p>@post.PublishedDate.ToString("MMMM dd, yyyy")</p>

@code {
    [Parameter] public int id { get; set; }
    private BlogPost post;

    protected override async Task OnInitializedAsync()
    {
        post = await blogService.GetPostByIdAsync(id);
    }
}
```

Step 4: Run the Application

Run the application and navigate to /blogs. You should see a list of blog posts with links to view each post in detail. You can also delete posts directly from the list, making this a fully functional blog application.

Key Takeaways

- **Entity Framework Core**: Provides a powerful and flexible way to interact with databases using C# objects and LINQ.
- **API Integration**: Using HttpClient, you can connect Blazor Server applications to external APIs to retrieve or send data.
- **CRUD Operations**: Essential for any data-driven application, CRUD operations in Blazor Server are simplified with EF Core's methods.
- **Hands-On Project**: The blog application showcases how these concepts can come together, enabling you to build complex, interactive applications.

Building Interactive and Real-Time Applications

B lazor Server stands out for its ability to create highly interactive applications without needing client-side JavaScript frameworks. Thanks to SignalR, Blazor Server can support real-time communication directly within C# components, enabling applications that can update users instantly. In this chapter, you'll learn to harness real-time features in Blazor Server, focusing on SignalR integration, component communication, and interactivity techniques that enhance responsiveness.

Introduction to SignalR and Real-Time Communication

SignalR is a .NET library that facilitates two-way, real-time communication between servers and clients. In Blazor Server, SignalR is integral to managing the connection between the server and the client, allowing for the efficient update of UI components based on real-time events.

How SignalR Works in Blazor Server

In Blazor Server applications, SignalR uses WebSockets (or other transport protocols as fallbacks) to establish a persistent connection between the server and client. This persistent connection allows for:

- **Push Notifications**: Server-sent updates that automatically reflect on the client side without requiring manual refreshes.
- **Two-Way Communication**: Both client and server can send and receive data, making it ideal for interactive features like chat, live dashboards,

and notifications.

- **Scalability**: SignalR allows Blazor Server apps to scale while handling multiple active connections, provided proper load balancing and state management are in place.

Understanding SignalR's role in Blazor Server helps you appreciate the seamless updates and interactions it enables, setting the foundation for building real-time applications.

Setting Up SignalR in Blazor Server

To integrate SignalR in a Blazor Server application, you first need to configure the server to recognize SignalR hubs, which are the components that manage communication between the client and server.

Step 1: Configure SignalR in Program.cs

Open Program.cs and add SignalR configuration to register the real-time communication hub:

- **Add SignalR to Services**:

```
builder.Services.AddSignalR();
```

- **Map the SignalR Hub Endpoint**: Add a map route for SignalR in the app.MapHub section:

```
app.MapHub<NotificationHub>("/notifications");
```

In this setup, /notifications is the URL endpoint clients will use to connect to the hub.

Step 2: Create the Notification Hub

In the **Hubs** folder, create a NotificationHub.cs class to define server-client communication methods.

NotificationHub.cs:

```
using Microsoft.AspNetCore.SignalR;
using System.Threading.Tasks;

public class NotificationHub : Hub
{
    public async Task SendNotification(string message)
    {
        await Clients.All.SendAsync("ReceiveNotification",
        message);
    }
}
```

In this example, SendNotification broadcasts a message to all connected clients using Clients.All.SendAsync.

Step 3: Creating a Real-Time Component to Handle Notifications

Next, create a NotificationComponent.razor component to handle incoming notifications from the hub.

- **Inject the IHubContext in the Component**:

```
@inject NavigationManager Navigation
@inject IHubContext<NotificationHub> NotificationHubContext
```

- **Initialize SignalR Connection and Event Handler**:

```
<div>
    <h3>Notifications</h3>
    <ul>
        @foreach (var notification in notifications)
```

```
        {
            <li>@notification</li>
        }
    </ul>
</div>

@code {
    private List<string> notifications = new List<string>();
    private HubConnection? hubConnection;

    protected override async Task OnInitializedAsync()
    {
        hubConnection = new HubConnectionBuilder()
            .WithUrl(Navigation.ToAbsoluteUri("/notifications"))
            .Build();

        hubConnection.On<string>("ReceiveNotification", (message)
        =>
        {
            notifications.Add(message);
            StateHasChanged();
        });

        await hubConnection.StartAsync();
    }

    public async ValueTask DisposeAsync()
    {
        if (hubConnection != null)
        {
            await hubConnection.DisposeAsync();
        }
    }
}
```

- **Explanation of Code**:
- OnInitializedAsync initializes the SignalR connection, subscribing to ReceiveNotification.

- notifications stores all incoming messages, and StateHasChanged() forces the UI to re-render when a new message arrives.

Testing the Setup

Run your app, open multiple browser tabs to simulate multiple clients, and manually invoke SendNotification from your backend. Each client should receive real-time notifications, proving that SignalR integration is working.

Component Communication and Interactivity

Managing communication between components is essential for interactive applications, especially in real-time environments. Blazor Server supports several patterns for component communication, including cascading values, dependency injection, and event callbacks.

Cascading Values and Parameters

Cascading values allow data to flow from a parent component to all of its descendants without explicit parameter passing, ideal for scenarios where shared data is frequently accessed across components.

Example:

- **Define a Cascading Value in a Parent Component**:

```
<CascadingValue Value="sharedMessage">
    <ChildComponent />
</CascadingValue>

@code {
    private string sharedMessage = "Real-Time Notification";
}
```

- **Access the Cascading Value in ChildComponent**:

```
@CascadingParameter
public string SharedMessage { get; set; }

<p>@SharedMessage</p>
```

Event Callbacks for Component-to-Parent Communication

Event callbacks allow child components to send data back to parent components, useful when a child component needs to trigger an update in its parent.

Example:

```
<ChildComponent OnNotify="HandleNotification" />

@code {
    private void HandleNotification(string message)
    {
        // Handle notification received from child component
    }
}
```

In this setup, OnNotify is an event callback that the child component can invoke to send notifications to the parent.

Real-Time Notification Dashboard Project

Let's build a real-time notification dashboard, combining SignalR, component communication, and interactive elements to create a feature-rich application.

Project Requirements

The notification dashboard will:

- Display incoming notifications in real-time.
- Allow users to clear notifications or filter by type.
- Use SignalR to broadcast messages from the server to all connected clients.

Step 1: Create the Notification Model

Define a Notification.cs class in the **Data** folder to represent each notification's properties.

Notification.cs:

```
public class Notification
{
    public string Message { get; set; }
    public DateTime Timestamp { get; set; }
    public string Type { get; set; } // e.g., "info", "warning",
    "error"
}
```

Step 2: Enhance the Notification Hub

Modify the NotificationHub to support broadcasting notifications with different types and timestamps.

NotificationHub.cs:

```
public class NotificationHub : Hub
{
    public async Task SendNotification(Notification notification)
    {
        await Clients.All.SendAsync("ReceiveNotification",
        notification);
    }
}
```

Step 3: Create a Real-Time Notification Component

In **Components**, create NotificationDashboard.razor.

- **Define the Markup and Code:**

```
@inject NavigationManager Navigation
@inject IHubContext<NotificationHub> NotificationHubContext

<div>
    <h3>Real-Time Notifications</h3>
    <button @onclick="ClearNotifications">Clear All</button>

    <ul>
        @foreach (var notification in notifications)
        {
            <li>
                <strong>@notification.Type</strong> -
                @notification.Message (Received at
                @notification.Timestamp)
            </li>
        }
    </ul>
</div>

@code {
    private List<Notification> notifications = new();
    private HubConnection? hubConnection;

    protected override async Task OnInitializedAsync()
    {
        hubConnection = new HubConnectionBuilder()
            .WithUrl(Navigation.ToAbsoluteUri("/notifications"))
            .Build();

        hubConnection.On<Notification>("ReceiveNotification",
        (notification) =>
        {
            notifications.Add(notification);
            StateHasChanged();
        });

        await hubConnection.StartAsync();
    }

    private void ClearNotifications() => notifications.Clear();
```

```
public async ValueTask DisposeAsync()
{
    if (hubConnection != null)
    {
        await hubConnection.DisposeAsync();
    }
}
}
```

- **Explanation of Code**:
- **Notifications List**: notifications stores received messages, each with a timestamp and type.
- **Clear Functionality**: The ClearNotifications method empties the list when triggered by a button.
- **Real-Time Data**: SignalR listens for incoming ReceiveNotification events, dynamically updating the UI.

Step 4: Testing the Dashboard

1. Run your application.
2. Open multiple tabs to simulate different users.
3. Use an administrative or backend trigger to send notifications, and watch as each client receives the update instantly.

This real-time notification dashboard demonstrates SignalR's power in live applications and provides a reusable foundation for building more complex interactive features.

Key Takeaways

- **SignalR Integration**: SignalR provides seamless, real-time two-way communication, allowing for interactive features without relying on client-side JavaScript.

- **Component Communication**: Techniques like cascading values and event callbacks enable data sharing and user-triggered updates across components, enhancing the interactivity of Blazor applications.
- **Real-Time Dashboard Project**: The notification dashboard highlights how SignalR and component communication come together to create responsive and interactive applications.

Authentication and Authorization in Blazor Server

A uthentication and authorization are two core concepts in web security:

- **Authentication** verifies a user's identity, often through login credentials like a username and password.
- **Authorization** determines what authenticated users can access based on their roles or permissions.

Blazor Server supports both authentication and authorization, enabling you to build secure applications by restricting access to components, pages, or specific actions.

Overview of Authentication in Blazor Server

Blazor Server apps typically use ASP.NET Core's authentication framework, which integrates seamlessly into Blazor. This framework offers flexibility in handling different authentication methods, including:

- **Cookie Authentication**: Common in traditional web applications, cookies store session data to keep users authenticated across requests.
- **JWT (JSON Web Tokens)**: Often used in APIs, JWT tokens are passed with each request, enabling stateless authentication.
- **OAuth/OpenID Connect**: Commonly used for third-party logins (e.g.,

Google, Facebook) and enterprise authentication (e.g., Azure AD).

In this chapter, we'll focus on cookie-based authentication, as it's well-suited to Blazor Server's stateful nature.

Setting Up Identity in Blazor Server

To handle user accounts, roles, and authentication, Blazor Server uses ASP.NET Core Identity, a powerful framework that provides built-in functionality for managing users and security.

- **Install ASP.NET Core Identity**: Open the NuGet Package Manager and install Microsoft.AspNetCore.Identity.EntityFrameworkCore and Microsoft.EntityFrameworkCore.SqlServer.
- **Configure Identity in Program.cs**: In Program.cs, add Identity services and set up Entity Framework with SQL Server (or another database provider):

```
builder.Services.AddDbContext<ApplicationDbContext>(options =>
    options.UseSqlServer("Your_Connection_String"));

builder.Services.AddIdentity<ApplicationUser, IdentityRole>()
    .AddEntityFrameworkStores<ApplicationDbContext>()
    .AddDefaultTokenProviders();

builder.Services.AddRazorPages();
builder.Services.AddServerSideBlazor();
```

- **Create an Identity Database Context**: Create an ApplicationDbConte xt.cs file in the **Data** folder to serve as the database context for Identity.

```
using Microsoft.AspNetCore.Identity;
using Microsoft.AspNetCore.Identity.EntityFrameworkCore;
```

```
using Microsoft.EntityFrameworkCore;

public class ApplicationDbContext :
IdentityDbContext<ApplicationUser>
{
    public
    ApplicationDbContext(DbContextOptions<ApplicationDbContext>
    options) : base(options) { }
}

public class ApplicationUser : IdentityUser
{
    // Additional user properties can be added here
}
```

Here, ApplicationUser represents the user model that Identity will manage, and you can add custom properties if needed.

- **Run Migrations to Create Identity Tables**: Use Entity Framework Core's migration commands to create the necessary database tables for Identity:

```
dotnet ef migrations add InitialIdentitySchema
dotnet ef database update
```

This setup will create tables for users, roles, and other security-related entities, providing a foundation for authentication.

Creating Authentication Pages

ASP.NET Core Identity provides default pages for user login, registration, and account management. However, for a more customized experience in Blazor, we'll create custom login and registration components.

Creating the Login Component

- **Create a Login.razor Component** in the **Pages** folder:

```razor
@page "/login"
@inject NavigationManager Navigation
@inject SignInManager<ApplicationUser> SignInManager

<EditForm Model="loginModel" OnValidSubmit="OnSubmit">
    <DataAnnotationsValidator />
    <ValidationSummary />

    <InputText @bind-Value="loginModel.Email" placeholder="Email"
    />
    <InputText @bind-Value="loginModel.Password"
    placeholder="Password" type="password" />
    <button type="submit">Login</button>
</EditForm>

@code {
    private LoginModel loginModel = new();

    private async Task OnSubmit()
    {
        var result = await
        SignInManager.PasswordSignInAsync(loginModel.Email,
        loginModel.Password, false, false);
        if (result.Succeeded)
        {
            Navigation.NavigateTo("/");
        }
        else
        {
            // Handle failed login
        }
    }

    public class LoginModel
    {
        public string Email { get; set; }
        public string Password { get; set; }
```

```
    }
}
```

- **Explanation of Code**:
- The SignInManager service is used to handle user login based on Identity.
- OnSubmit checks the login credentials and redirects to the home page on success.

Creating the Registration Component

- **Create a Register.razor Component**:

```
@page "/register"
@inject UserManager<ApplicationUser> UserManager
@inject SignInManager<ApplicationUser> SignInManager
@inject NavigationManager Navigation

<EditForm Model="registerModel" OnValidSubmit="OnRegister">
    <DataAnnotationsValidator />
    <ValidationSummary />

    <InputText @bind-Value="registerModel.Email"
    placeholder="Email" />
    <InputText @bind-Value="registerModel.Password"
    placeholder="Password" type="password" />
    <InputText @bind-Value="registerModel.ConfirmPassword"
    placeholder="Confirm Password" type="password" />
    <button type="submit">Register</button>
</EditForm>

@code {
    private RegisterModel registerModel = new();

    private async Task OnRegister()
    {
```

```
        var user = new ApplicationUser { UserName =
        registerModel.Email, Email = registerModel.Email };
        var result = await UserManager.CreateAsync(user,
        registerModel.Password);
        if (result.Succeeded)
        {
            await SignInManager.SignInAsync(user, isPersistent:
            false);
            Navigation.NavigateTo("/");
        }
        else
        {
            // Handle registration failure
        }
    }

    public class RegisterModel
    {
        public string Email { get; set; }
        public string Password { get; set; }
        public string ConfirmPassword { get; set; }
    }
}
```

- **Explanation of Code**:
- The UserManager service handles user creation, while SignInManager manages login.
- Upon successful registration, the user is signed in and redirected to the home page.

Role-Based Authorization in Blazor Server

Roles allow you to assign permissions to users and control access based on these roles. ASP.NET Core Identity supports role-based authorization out of the box, which can be implemented in Blazor with role checks and policy-based requirements.

Creating Roles in the Database

Roles can be created directly in the database or programmatically. Here's how to create roles programmatically at application startup.

- **Add Role Creation Code in Program.cs**:

```
using Microsoft.AspNetCore.Identity;

var serviceProvider = builder.Services.BuildServiceProvider();
var roleManager =
serviceProvider.GetRequiredService<RoleManager<IdentityRole>>();

var roles = new[] { "Admin", "User" };
foreach (var role in roles)
{
    if (!await roleManager.RoleExistsAsync(role))
    {
        await roleManager.CreateAsync(new IdentityRole(role));
    }
}
```

- **Assign a Role to a User**: You can assign a role to a user programmatically as follows:

```
var user = await UserManager.FindByEmailAsync("user@example.com");
await UserManager.AddToRoleAsync(user, "Admin");
```

With roles defined, you can begin restricting content in Blazor based on user roles.

Restricting Access to Components and Pages

- **Using AuthorizeView for Role-Based Display**: Blazor's Authorize-View component conditionally renders content based on user roles.

Example:

```
<AuthorizeView Roles="Admin">
    <h3>Admin Dashboard</h3>
    <p>Only users with the Admin role can see this content.</p>
</AuthorizeView>
```

- **Protecting Entire Pages with @attribute [Authorize]**: To secure an entire page, use the @attribute directive with [Authorize]. For instance, in AdminPage.razor:

```
@page "/admin"
@attribute [Authorize(Roles = "Admin")]

<h3>Admin Panel</h3>
<p>This page is restricted to Admin users only.</p>
```

This approach ensures only authorized users can access specific routes or sections of the app, providing fine-grained access control.

Project: Adding Authentication to a Blog Application

To solidify your understanding, let's implement basic authentication and authorization in the blog application developed in previous chapters. In this project, only authenticated users will be able to create, edit, and delete blog posts, while any visitor can view them.

Project Requirements

The blog application will:

- Allow users to register and log in.
- Restrict post creation, editing, and deletion to logged-in users.
- Limit admin-level actions (such as deleting posts) to users with the Admin role.

Step 1: Update Blog Components with Authorization

- **Restrict Access to the Blog Editor**: Wrap the editor component in an AuthorizeView to ensure only logged-in users can see it.

```
<AuthorizeView>
    <Authorized>
        <!-- Blog editor code goes here -->
    </Authorized>
    <NotAuthorized>
        <p>Please log in to add or edit posts.</p>
    </NotAuthorized>
</AuthorizeView>
```

- **Admin-Only Delete Functionality**: Limit delete functionality to users in the Admin role:

```
<AuthorizeView Roles="Admin">
    <button @onclick="() => DeletePost(post.Id)">Delete</button>
</AuthorizeView>
```

Step 2: Secure Backend Services

In the BlogService (or wherever sensitive logic is executed), you can add role-based checks to protect your server-side operations:

```
public async Task DeletePostAsync(int id, ClaimsPrincipal user)
{
    if (!user.IsInRole("Admin"))
    {
        throw new UnauthorizedAccessException("Only admins can
        delete posts.");
    }
```

```
var post = await dbContext.BlogPosts.FindAsync(id);
if (post != null)
{
    dbContext.BlogPosts.Remove(post);
    await dbContext.SaveChangesAsync();
}
}
```

This additional check enforces security even if the client-side restrictions are bypassed, which is essential for robust authorization.

Key Takeaways

- **Authentication**: ASP.NET Core Identity integrates well with Blazor Server to provide login, registration, and session management features.
- **Role-Based Authorization**: Use roles to restrict access to specific components or pages, ensuring users can only access what they're permitted to.
- **Secure Backend Services**: Reinforce client-side security with role checks on the server side to prevent unauthorized access to sensitive operations.

Enhancing Performance and Scalability

A
s with any web application, Blazor Server applications benefit from performance and scalability enhancements that make the user experience smoother and enable your app to handle larger volumes of traffic. In Blazor Server, where UI updates are processed on the server and sent to the client in real-time, optimizing how data is loaded and rendered, managing the server-client connection efficiently, and reducing resource consumption are key to achieving high performance.

Understanding Blazor Server's Unique Performance Challenges

Blazor Server apps operate on a persistent connection between the client and server, where all UI updates are processed server-side and communicated via SignalR. This architecture introduces specific challenges:

1. **Server Load**: Each client maintains an active connection to the server, so every interaction adds load to the server.
2. **Network Latency**: All interactions involve data transfer between the client and server, which means the app's responsiveness depends on network speed and latency.
3. **Rendering Efficiency**: As components re-render, they can introduce processing overhead if not managed efficiently, especially with complex or frequently updated UIs.

Optimizing for these challenges involves improving rendering efficiency, minimizing network requests, and carefully managing server resources.

Optimizing Component Rendering

In Blazor Server, component rendering directly impacts server performance. Efficient rendering means that only the necessary UI updates are processed and sent to the client.

Using ShouldRender to Control Rendering

By default, Blazor re-renders components whenever their state changes. However, you can override the ShouldRender method to control when re-rendering occurs, preventing unnecessary updates.

Example:

```
@code {
    private int counter = 0;

    protected override bool ShouldRender()
    {
        return counter % 2 == 0; // Only render when counter is
        even
    }

    private void Increment()
    {
        counter++;
    }
}
```

In this example, the component will only re-render when counter is even, reducing unnecessary rendering cycles.

Avoiding Large Component Re-Renders

Complex components with numerous child elements can become performance bottlenecks if they frequently re-render. One solution is to split large components into smaller, independent components that render individually.

1. **Divide Components**: Break down large components into smaller ones, each responsible for a specific part of the UI.
2. **Use @key Directive**: The @key directive can help Blazor optimize rendering by associating elements with unique keys, allowing it to track

individual items in collections.

Example:

```
@foreach (var item in Items)
{
    <div @key="item.Id">
        @item.Name
    </div>
}
```

With @key, Blazor identifies elements in a collection, minimizing DOM manipulation and enhancing performance during re-renders.

Efficient Data Loading

Data fetching is often the biggest contributor to slow page loads. In Blazor Server, this can be mitigated through techniques like lazy loading, pre-rendering, and caching data.

Lazy Loading and On-Demand Data Fetching

Lazy loading involves loading data only when needed, rather than upfront. This can reduce initial load time and improve perceived performance.

- **Load Data in Chunks**: For large datasets, consider loading data in pages or chunks. For example, a product catalog might only load the first 20 items initially and fetch more as the user scrolls.

Example:

```
@code {
    private List<Product> products = new List<Product>();
    private int pageNumber = 1;

    protected override async Task OnInitializedAsync()
    {
```

```
        products = await LoadProducts(pageNumber);
    }

    private async Task LoadMore()
    {
        pageNumber++;
        var moreProducts = await LoadProducts(pageNumber);
        products.AddRange(moreProducts);
    }
}
```

- **Use On-Demand Loading in UI**: Trigger additional data loads when the user scrolls or navigates to a new section, rather than preloading everything.

Data Pre-Rendering

Pre-rendering allows you to load data before it's displayed on the screen, enhancing performance for content-heavy pages. Blazor's OnParametersSetAsync and OnInitializedAsync lifecycle methods enable data loading before components render, improving user experience.

Example:

```
protected override async Task OnInitializedAsync()
{
    data = await FetchDataAsync();
}
```

This approach is especially useful for components that require data to be available immediately after loading.

Caching for Improved Performance

Caching can help reduce server load by reusing previously fetched data instead of re-fetching it from the database or an external API.

Memory Caching

In Blazor Server, MemoryCache allows you to store data in memory for a specified duration, minimizing redundant database queries or API calls.

- **Register MemoryCache** in Program.cs:

```
builder.Services.AddMemoryCache();
```

- **Use MemoryCache in Components**:

```
@inject IMemoryCache cache

@code {
    private List<Product> products;

    protected override async Task OnInitializedAsync()
    {
        if (!cache.TryGetValue("Products", out products))
        {
            products = await FetchProductsAsync();
            cache.Set("Products", products,
            TimeSpan.FromMinutes(10));
        }
    }
}
```

In this example, products are cached for 10 minutes, reducing the need to reload data frequently.

Client-Side Caching

For data that doesn't need to be real-time, client-side caching with local storage or session storage can provide even faster access and reduce server requests.

Optimizing SignalR and Managing Server Load

SignalR is at the core of Blazor Server's real-time communication, but each connection consumes server resources. Optimizing SignalR usage is crucial for applications with high user activity.

Connection Management

SignalR connections can strain server resources, so managing connections actively is key.

1. **Close Idle Connections**: Set a timeout for inactive users to disconnect after a period of inactivity.
2. **Scale with SignalR**: Consider configuring SignalR to use Redis or Azure SignalR Service if you anticipate high traffic. This can improve scalability by distributing the load across multiple servers.

Reducing Network Overhead

Network bandwidth is a significant factor in real-time applications. Minimizing data sent between server and client can help reduce load.

1. **Use Lightweight Data**: Avoid sending large payloads over SignalR. Instead, send only the necessary data for UI updates.
2. **Optimize State Tracking**: Blazor maintains a component state across each SignalR connection. Avoid storing large objects in component state to reduce the memory footprint on the server.

State Management Techniques

Blazor Server maintains component state across the SignalR connection, which can increase memory usage as the number of users grows. Effective state management helps mitigate this.

Application-Level State Management

Storing application state globally in a singleton service can reduce memory usage per session. For instance, user preferences or frequently accessed data can be stored centrally rather than per component.

- **Create a Singleton Service**:

```
public class AppState
{
    public string UserName { get; set; }
}
```

- **Register in Program.cs**:

```
builder.Services.AddSingleton<AppState>();
```

Using singletons minimizes memory usage by reducing the need for duplicated data across sessions.

Session-Based State Management

For data that must persist per user session, use ProtectedSessionStorage, which provides secure, per-session storage.

Scalable Product Catalog Project

Let's put these performance techniques into practice by building a product catalog that's optimized for scalability and efficient data access. The catalog will use lazy loading, caching, and efficient state management to minimize load on the server.

Project Requirements

The scalable product catalog will:

- Load product data in chunks as the user scrolls.
- Cache product data to reduce database queries.
- Use a singleton state service to manage shared data across components.

Step 1: Define the Product Model

In the **Data** folder, create Product.cs to define each product's attributes.
Product.cs:

```
public class Product
{
    public int Id { get; set; }
    public string Name { get; set; }
    public string Description { get; set; }
    public decimal Price { get; set; }
}
```

Step 2: Create the Product Service with Caching

Create ProductService.cs in the **Services** folder to manage product data, using memory caching to reduce database calls.

ProductService.cs:

```
public class ProductService
{
    private readonly IMemoryCache _cache;

    public ProductService(IMemoryCache cache)
    {
        _cache = cache;
    }

    public async Task<List<Product>> GetProductsAsync(int page)
    {
        if (!_cache.TryGetValue("ProductsPage" + page, out
        List<Product> products))
        {
            products = await FetchProductsFromDb(page); //
            Simulated database call
            _cache.Set("ProductsPage" + page, products,
            TimeSpan.FromMinutes(10));
        }
```

return products; } }

```
##### **Step 3: Build the Product Catalog Component**
```

Create `ProductCatalog.razor` to display products with lazy loading.

ProductCatalog.razor:
```razor
@inject ProductService productService
<h3>Product Catalog</h3>

<div>
    @foreach (var product in products)
    {
        <div>@product.Name - @product.Price</div>
    }
</div>

<button @onclick="LoadMore">Load More</button>

@code {
    private List<Product> products = new List<Product>();
    private int page = 1;

    protected override async Task OnInitializedAsync()
    {
        products = await productService.GetProductsAsync(page);
    }

    private async Task LoadMore()
    {
        page++;
        var moreProducts = await
        productService.GetProductsAsync(page);
        products.AddRange(moreProducts);
    }
}
```

Step 4: Test for Scalability

Run the application, load initial products, and use Load More to fetch additional data. Verify that data loads smoothly without overwhelming the server, thanks to caching and lazy loading.

Key Takeaways

- **Component Optimization**: Efficient rendering minimizes re-renders and reduces server load.
- **Efficient Data Loading**: Lazy loading and pre-rendering prevent initial load bottlenecks and improve the perceived speed.
- **Caching**: Memory caching and client-side storage reduce redundant data fetching, boosting performance.
- **SignalR and State Management**: Optimizing SignalR usage and managing state efficiently allow for scalable, interactive applications.

Integrating with the .NET Ecosystem

Blazor Server's strength lies in its deep integration with .NET, allowing developers to leverage the entire ecosystem to build robust applications. This integration simplifies the development process, from data access and real-time functionalities to deploying and monitoring applications. Understanding how to harness these capabilities can significantly enhance your Blazor Server applications.

Using ASP.NET Core Features

Blazor Server is built on ASP.NET Core, which provides a wealth of features that can be leveraged directly within Blazor applications. These include middleware, configuration systems, dependency injection, and more.

Middleware Integration

ASP.NET Core's middleware pipeline is a powerful mechanism for handling HTTP requests and responses. Blazor Server apps can utilize custom middleware for tasks such as authentication, logging, or custom headers.

Example: Adding a simple logging middleware.

```
public void Configure(IApplicationBuilder app)
{
    app.UseMiddleware<LoggingMiddleware>();
    app.UseEndpoints(endpoints =>
    {
        endpoints.MapBlazorHub();
        endpoints.MapFallbackToPage("/_Host");
    });
```

```
}

public class LoggingMiddleware
{
    private readonly RequestDelegate _next;

    public LoggingMiddleware(RequestDelegate next)
    {
        _next = next;
    }

    public async Task InvokeAsync(HttpContext context)
    {
        // Log request path
        Console.WriteLine("Handling request: " +
        context.Request.Path);
        await _next(context);
        // Log response status
        Console.WriteLine("Finished handling request.");
    }
}
```

This middleware logs the path of each request and the status after processing, showcasing how middleware can be utilized within a Blazor Server application.

Dependency Injection

Blazor leverages ASP.NET Core's built-in dependency injection (DI) container, which can be used to manage services and their lifetimes throughout the application.

Example: Configuring DI to use a scoped service.

```
public void ConfigureServices(IServiceCollection services)
{
    services.AddScoped<IProductService, ProductService>();
}
```

In this example, IProductService is injected into Blazor components, ensuring that a new instance is provided for each connection, which is particularly useful in scenarios like data access where scope management is crucial.

Integrating Entity Framework Core

Entity Framework Core (EF Core) is the preferred ORM for .NET developers due to its efficiency and developer-friendly API. Integrating EF Core with Blazor Server allows for robust data management.

Configuring EF Core

To integrate EF Core, you must first define your data model and DbContext.

Example: Setting up a DbContext.

```
public class ApplicationDbContext : DbContext
{
    public ApplicationDbContext(DbContextOptions
<ApplicationDbContext> options)
        : base(options)
    {
    }

    public DbSet<Product> Products { get; set; }
}
```

Next, configure the connection string and register the DbContext in Program.cs.

```
services.AddDbContext
<ApplicationDbContext>(options =>
    options.UseSqlServer(Configuration.
GetConnectionString
("DefaultConnection")));
```

Using EF Core in Components

EF Core can be injected directly into Blazor components using DI.

Example: Accessing data in a component.

```
@inject ApplicationDbContext DbContext

<h1>Products</h1>

@if (products == null)
{
    <p><em>Loading...</em></p>
}
else
{
    foreach (var product in products)
    {
        <p>@product.Name</p>
    }
}

@code {
    private List<Product> products;

    protected override async Task OnInitializedAsync()
    {
        products = await DbContext.Products.ToListAsync();
    }
}
```

This component loads products from the database when initialized, demonstrating how EF Core can be seamlessly integrated into Blazor components for data access.

Real-Time Communication with SignalR

SignalR, which is already part of Blazor Server's underlying infrastructure, can also be used more explicitly to add real-time web functionalities to your applications, such as chat features or live updates.

Example: Creating a chat component.

```
@inject IHubContext<ChatHub> ChatHubContext

<input @bind="message" />
<button @onclick="SendMessage">Send</button>

@code {
    private string message;

    private async Task SendMessage()
    {
        await ChatHubContext.Clients.All.
SendAsync("ReceiveMessage", message);
        message = string.Empty;
    }
}
```

In this example, ChatHub is used to send messages in real-time to all connected clients, showcasing SignalR's capabilities within a Blazor context.

Integrating with Azure Services

Azure provides various services that can enhance the capabilities of your Blazor Server applications, including Azure SQL Database, Azure Functions, and Azure SignalR Service.

Using Azure SignalR Service

For applications requiring high scalability, integrating Azure SignalR Service can offload the connection management from your servers.

Example: Configuring Azure SignalR Service.

```
public void ConfigureServices(IServiceCollection services)
{
    services.AddSignalR().
AddAzureSignalR("Your_Connection_String");
}
```

This setup allows your Blazor app to scale more effectively by utilizing Azure's managed infrastructure.

Project: Building a Sales Dashboard with .NET Integrations

Finally, let's build a sales dashboard that integrates multiple ASP.NET services, demonstrating the capabilities of the .NET ecosystem in a Blazor Server application.

Project Requirements

The dashboard will:

- Display real-time sales data.
- Use EF Core for data storage.
- Use SignalR for live updates.
- Incorporate Azure services for scalability and data handling.

Step 1: Set Up the Data Model and DbContext

Define your models and DbContext as previously shown, ensuring your database is properly configured for the data you need to display.

Step 2: Create Real-Time Data Updates with SignalR

Configure SignalR to send updates to clients whenever sales data changes, ensuring all users see the most up-to-date information.

Step 3: Implement Azure Services for Scalability

Configure Azure SignalR Service and possibly Azure Functions to handle data processing, reducing the load on your main application server and improving responsiveness.

Step 4: Develop the UI with Blazor

Build the UI components that display sales data, using Blazor's data binding and component features to create an interactive, real-time user experience.

Key Takeaways

- **ASP.NET Core Features**: Leverage middleware, DI, and more to enhance application functionality and maintainability.
- **Entity Framework Core**: Use EF Core for robust data handling.
- **SignalR**: Implement real-time communication for interactive features.
- **Azure Services**: Utilize Azure's managed services to scale and enhance

your Blazor applications.

Common Pitfalls, Best Practices, and Troubleshooting

Blazor Server is a powerful framework with distinct advantages, but it also has unique challenges. Because Blazor Server applications depend on continuous server-client connections and server-side rendering, understanding potential pitfalls and following best practices is essential to building stable, performant, and user-friendly applications. This chapter provides a guide to avoiding common issues, recommended practices, and techniques for troubleshooting when things go wrong.

Common Pitfalls in Blazor Server

Blazor Server's architecture and connection-based design introduce specific challenges that can impact performance, scalability, and user experience. Here are some common pitfalls to watch out for:

1. Overuse of Large Components and Frequent Re-renders

When a component's state changes, it triggers a re-render, which can lead to performance degradation if the component is large or complex. This can be especially problematic in Blazor Server, where re-renders mean more data sent across the network.

Solution:

- **Break Down Components**: Split large components into smaller, focused components that manage specific parts of the UI. This reduces unnecessary re-renders for the entire page.

- **Use ShouldRender**: Override the ShouldRender method to control when re-renders happen, only allowing updates when necessary.

2. Poor State Management Across Components

When managing data in Blazor Server, it's tempting to rely on component-level state. However, this approach can lead to issues with data synchronization and memory consumption, particularly in complex applications.
Solution:

- **Use Singleton or Scoped Services**: Store global application data in services, such as singleton services, injected using dependency injection. This allows components to share and access the same data without duplicating memory usage.

3. Inefficient Data Loading and API Calls

Fetching all data at once can slow down page loads, while making too many network requests can overwhelm both server and client resources.
Solution:

- **Implement Lazy Loading**: Load only the data needed at the time, such as fetching only the first page of a dataset and loading more as the user interacts.
- **Cache Data**: Use caching for frequently requested data to reduce repetitive network calls and database queries.

4. Failing to Dispose of Resources

Blazor components can open up unmanaged resources like database connections or network streams. Failure to release these resources can lead to memory leaks and resource exhaustion.
Solution:

- **Implement IDisposable**: Ensure components that hold unmanaged resources implement IDisposable and release resources in Dispose().

5. Unhandled Exceptions and Lack of Error Feedback

Unhandled exceptions can disrupt user experience and leave users without guidance. Blazor Server applications can encounter connection issues, server errors, or application exceptions that need to be handled gracefully.

Solution:

- **Centralized Error Handling**: Set up error-handling middleware to capture errors and display user-friendly messages.
- **Use Error Boundaries**: Leverage Blazor's error boundary features to isolate failures and display custom error messages to users.

Best Practices for Blazor Server Development

Following best practices can help you build scalable, maintainable, and efficient Blazor Server applications. Here are some recommended approaches:

1. Optimize Data Binding and Component Updates

Data binding is a core feature of Blazor, but overusing it can impact performance if used on frequently updating fields.

Recommendation:

- **Use @bind Judiciously**: Limit data binding to necessary fields. For example, avoid two-way binding on fields that don't need to propagate updates back to the server in real-time.

2. Use SignalR Wisely

Blazor Server relies on SignalR for real-time client-server communication. Although powerful, SignalR connections consume resources, so managing them wisely is key to scalability.

Recommendation:

- **Limit Connection Lifetime**: Automatically disconnect inactive users after a period of inactivity.
- **Use Lightweight Payloads**: Minimize data sent over SignalR to reduce network load.

3. Implement Robust State Management

State management is crucial in applications where data is shared across components or pages. Avoid storing large state objects within components themselves.

Recommendation:

- **Store Application-Level Data in Services**: Use scoped or singleton services to handle shared state across components.
- **Use ProtectedSessionStorage or LocalStorage for Per-User Data**: For user-specific data that needs persistence, consider using session or local storage.

4. Leverage Dependency Injection for Testability and Maintainability

Dependency injection (DI) simplifies testing and improves maintainability by allowing services to be swapped out easily.

Recommendation:

- **Register Services with DI Container**: Use DI to register application services, following the recommended lifetimes (e.g., singleton, scoped).
- **Inject Dependencies**: Avoid direct instantiation of services in components; instead, inject them to improve testability.

5. Enhance User Experience with Error Boundaries

Error boundaries in Blazor Server can help you gracefully handle component-level errors, which is particularly useful in complex or dynamic applications.

Recommendation:

- **Use Error Boundaries**: Surround components that may fail with an error boundary to isolate issues and present user-friendly error messages.
- **Log Errors**: Log errors in a central location, such as a logging service, for monitoring and debugging.

Troubleshooting Common Issues in Blazor Server

Troubleshooting Blazor Server issues requires understanding of both the Blazor framework and ASP.NET Core. Here's how to address common issues that developers encounter.

1. Debugging Component Re-Renders

If a component is re-rendering too frequently, it can lead to performance issues.

Solution:

- **Check Data Binding**: Examine @bind statements to ensure you aren't binding to values that change too frequently.
- **Use ShouldRender Method**: Override ShouldRender to restrict unnecessary renders.

2. Handling Connection-Related Issues

Blazor Server relies on a persistent SignalR connection. Connection issues can cause components to stop responding or disconnect entirely.

Solution:

- **Set Up Reconnection Logic**: Configure Blazor's automatic reconnection options in Program.cs to manage temporary disconnections.

```
builder.Services.AddServerSideBlazor()
    .AddCircuitOptions(options => {
    options.JSInteropDefaultCallTimeout = TimeSpan.FromMinutes(3);
    });
```

- **Monitor Connection Status**: Use the @onconnectionchange event to detect disconnections and alert users accordingly.

3. Fixing Memory Leaks from Unmanaged Resources

Memory leaks can arise if components with unmanaged resources aren't

disposed of properly.
Solution:

- **Use DisposeAsync**: Implement IDisposable or IAsyncDisposable for components that use unmanaged resources, ensuring resources are cleaned up when the component is removed.
- **Avoid Stateful Singletons**: If using singletons, ensure they don't hold state that grows indefinitely, as this can lead to memory bloat.

4. Addressing Authentication and Authorization Issues

In applications with protected routes, users may experience issues accessing restricted pages if authorization isn't correctly configured.
Solution:

- **Verify Authentication Setup**: Check that authentication middleware and authorization policies are correctly configured in Program.cs.
- **Test User Roles**: Ensure users have the correct roles or permissions for restricted actions, as incorrect configuration can prevent access.

5. Handling Slow Data Loading

Slow data loading can negatively impact the user experience, particularly in data-heavy applications.
Solution:

- **Implement Lazy Loading**: Load data in small chunks and only fetch additional data as needed.
- **Optimize Database Queries**: Profile database queries to eliminate inefficiencies, and consider caching data that is frequently accessed.

Best Practices Summary

To create high-performing, maintainable Blazor Server applications, consider these best practices as a checklist:

1. **Component Structure**: Keep components small and focused, and use ShouldRender to control re-renders.
2. **State Management**: Use DI for shared state, and consider scoped or singleton services for per-session data.
3. **Efficient Data Loading**: Use lazy loading and caching to optimize database access and improve page load times.
4. **Error Handling**: Set up error boundaries, centralized logging, and user-friendly error messages to handle exceptions gracefully.
5. **SignalR Optimization**: Minimize SignalR data payloads and automatically disconnect inactive sessions to save resources.

Advanced Topics and Beyond

B lazor Server offers robust functionality out of the box, but advanced techniques can elevate your application's quality, performance, and maintainability. In this chapter, we'll focus on advanced features and scenarios, empowering you to build enterprise-level applications that are maintainable, scalable, and optimized for modern web requirements.

Deploying and Scaling Blazor Server Applications

Deployment is a crucial aspect of production-ready Blazor Server applications, especially for applications expecting high traffic or requiring global reach. Blazor Server's reliance on server resources makes efficient deployment and scaling strategies essential for maintaining responsiveness.

Deploying to Azure App Service

Azure App Service provides a scalable, managed hosting solution that works well with Blazor Server.

- **Set Up an App Service**:
- Use the Azure portal to create a new App Service and configure it with your desired settings (region, OS, and pricing tier).
- **Publish from Visual Studio**:
- In Visual Studio, right-click your Blazor Server project, select **Publish**, choose **Azure**, and select the App Service you created.

Azure App Service automatically handles scaling and load balancing, making it easy to manage traffic spikes and ensure reliability.

Scaling Considerations

To optimize for high traffic, consider these scaling strategies:

- **SignalR with Azure SignalR Service**: Offloading SignalR traffic to Azure SignalR Service improves scalability and reduces server load by distributing real-time connections.
- **Load Balancing**: Use load balancers to distribute traffic across multiple instances, which is particularly helpful for maintaining high availability.
- **Geo-Distribution**: Deploy instances in multiple regions for faster response times, especially for globally distributed users.

Building Reusable Component Libraries

Reusable component libraries streamline development by allowing you to share components across projects or within development teams. With .NET's class library support, you can create, publish, and manage component libraries like any other package.

Creating a Component Library

- **Create a Razor Class Library (RCL)**:
- In Visual Studio, add a new **Razor Class Library** project to your solution. This library is specifically designed for building reusable Blazor components.
- **Add Components to the Library**:
- Add .razor components to the library project just as you would in a Blazor application project.

Using Component Libraries in Applications

To use a component library in a Blazor Server app:

- **Add a Reference to the Library**:
- Right-click on your Blazor Server project, select **Add Reference**, and choose the Razor Class Library.
- **Use the Library Components**:

- Import the library's namespace in your app's _Imports.razor file and use the components as you would any other.

This approach is ideal for developing standardized, consistent UI components that can be reused across applications, reducing duplication and speeding up development.

JavaScript Interoperability (JS Interop)

Blazor Server can integrate with JavaScript, enabling access to functionality that isn't natively available in .NET. JS Interop is useful for interacting with browser-specific features, third-party JavaScript libraries, or custom scripts.

Calling JavaScript from C#

To call a JavaScript function from C#:

- **Define a JavaScript Function**:
- In wwwroot, add a JavaScript file (e.g., scripts.js) and define your function:

```
function showAlert(message) {
    alert(message);
}
```

- **Register JavaScript in _Host.cshtml**:
- Add a reference to your JavaScript file in the _Host.cshtml layout file.

```
<script src="scripts.js"></script>
```

- **Call JavaScript from a Blazor Component**:
- Use the IJSRuntime service to call the JavaScript function:

```
@inject IJSRuntime JS

<button @onclick="ShowAlert">Show Alert</button>

@code {
    private async Task ShowAlert()
    {
        await JS.InvokeVoidAsync("showAlert", "Hello from
        Blazor!");
    }
}
```

Calling .NET from JavaScript

To call a .NET method from JavaScript:

- ### Define a .NET Method with [JSInvokable]:

```
[JSInvokable]
public static Task<string> GetMessageFromDotNet()
{
    return Task.FromResult("Hello from .NET!");
}
```

- ### Call the Method from JavaScript:

```
DotNet.invokeMethodAsync('YourAssemblyName',
'GetMessageFromDotNet')
    .then(data => console.log(data));
```

JS Interop provides flexibility, enabling you to create interactive, modern user experiences by bridging Blazor with JavaScript functionality.

Adding Unit and Integration Testing

Testing is essential for maintaining quality in large or complex Blazor Server applications. Unit testing allows you to verify individual components and services, while integration testing ensures that different parts of the application work together correctly.

Unit Testing Components

To create a unit test for a Blazor component, use a testing framework such as **xUnit** and a Blazor testing library like **bUnit**.

- **Set Up bUnit**:
- Add the bUnit NuGet package to your test project:

```
dotnet add package bunit
```

- **Write a Test for a Component**:

```
public class CounterTests
{
    [Fact]
    public void Counter_Increments_WhenClicked()
    {
        using var context = new TestContext();
        var component = context.RenderComponent<Counter>();

        // Act - find and click the button
        component.Find("button").Click();

        // Assert - verify counter incremented
        Assert.Equal("Current count: 1",
        component.Find("p").TextContent);
    }
}
```

In this test, bUnit is used to render the Counter component, simulate a button click, and verify that the counter text updated correctly.

Integration Testing

Integration testing in Blazor Server can be set up using ASP.NET Core's test server, which enables you to spin up a test instance of your Blazor app.

- **Create a Test Project**:
- Add a new test project and reference Microsoft.AspNetCore.Mvc.Testing.
- **Write an Integration Test**:

```
public class AppTests :
IClassFixture<WebApplicationFactory<Startup>>
{
    private readonly HttpClient _client;

    public AppTests(WebApplicationFactory<Startup> factory)
    {
        _client = factory.CreateClient();
    }

    [Fact]
    public async Task HomePage_LoadsSuccessfully()
    {
        var response = await _client.GetAsync("/");
        response.EnsureSuccessStatusCode();
    }
}
```

This test verifies that the home page loads without errors, ensuring basic application functionality. Integration testing helps catch issues that could arise from misconfigurations or dependencies between services.

Where to Go Next? Resources for Continued Learning

Blazor Server is part of the fast-evolving .NET ecosystem, with new features, libraries, and integrations emerging frequently. Here are some recommended resources and areas for further exploration:

- **Official Microsoft Documentation**:
- The official Blazor documentation on Microsoft's website is updated regularly and provides detailed guides, tutorials, and reference material.
- **ASP.NET Core Community**:
- The ASP.NET Core community provides blog posts, video tutorials, and open-source projects that showcase Blazor best practices and advanced techniques.
- **Blazor University and bUnit Documentation**:
- Blazor University offers free, in-depth tutorials and examples on Blazor topics. The bUnit documentation covers all aspects of Blazor component testing.
- **Popular Blazor Libraries**:
- Libraries like MudBlazor (for Material Design components) and Blazored (for utilities) add functionality to Blazor projects. These libraries often have strong community support and are updated regularly.
- **Experiment with Hybrid Models**:
- Explore Blazor Hybrid apps, which enable Blazor components to run within native desktop applications using technologies like .NET MAUI. This is an exciting area for developers looking to use Blazor outside the browser.
- **Learn Cloud-Native Blazor**:
- Blazor's cloud-native applications can leverage Azure Functions, Kubernetes, and other microservice architectures. Learning about these options can make your applications more scalable and resilient.